Revelations of INFINITE LIFE

Flaming Gems of Wisdom for your Spiritual Journey

Dr. S. Wesley Abraham

RITERA PUBLISHING

Revelations of Infinite Life
Flaming Gems of Wisdom for your Spiritual Journey

ISBN: 978-81-984984-5-8
First Edition

Revelations of GLORY… GAIN… GOLD…

-Dr. Wesley Abraham

Contents

About the Author

A Legacy of Faith, Excellence, and Transformation

Apostle Dr. Wesley Abraham in Chennai, India, to Mr. and Mrs. Sikkandar Raj David, is an inspiring legend whose life blends professional excellence with profound spiritual influence. Married to Grace Mercy Wesley, they are blessed with two gifts from Above - little princess Joanna Gloria Wesley and prince John Giuda Wesley. His life is a profound testimony of faith, purpose, and the transformative power of the Holy Spirit. A man of many talents, he has dedicated his life to advancing God's Kingdom while excelling in every role he has undertaken.

Academic and Professional Journey

Dr. Wesley Abraham's foundational years were spent in Chennai, where he completed his schooling. He graduated with distinction, earning a B.Tech in Information Technology from Anna University, where he also served as the Student Chairman. His academic pursuits continued with an MBA in Human Resources from the University of Madras, graduating with first-class honors. He achieved the distinguished honor of a Doctorate in Ministry. Additionally, he holds the titles *Hindi Pandit* and *Pracharak* from the Dakshina Bharat Hindi Prachar Sabha, equivalent to a Bachelor of Arts in Hindi.

Professionally, Dr. Wesley Abraham built a remarkable career in the IT sector, working across industries such as banking, healthcare, and web domains. Over his 12-year career, he collaborated with prominent organizations, and over 2,000 financial institutions in the U.S. His expertise in software technologies and dedication to excellence earned him recognition as a key contributor to numerous successful projects. While he built an impeccable career as a software engineer, demonstrating exceptional faithfulness, integrity, and professionalism, his true calling lay beyond the corporate world.

Early Calling and Ministry

Dr. Wesley Abraham's spiritual journey began at the tender age of five, when he delivered his first sermon on faith. His divine calling led him to serve as a preacher, songwriter, worship leader and prophetic minister. From directing Sunday schools to leading youth ministries, Dr. Wesley Abraham has embraced diverse roles in ministry, all driven by his unwavering commitment to fulfilling God's purpose. In 2006, he founded *Crystals of Christ (COC)*, a children's ministry that grew from nine students to over 100, marking the start of his impactful ministry work.

Ministry and Leadership

Dr. Wesley Abraham is the founder of ***Forever Life International Ministries*** serving globally through Spirit-filled teaching and outreach, pioneered a group of diverse ministry initiatives, including:

1. **Keba Fellowship**

    - A Heavenly factory producing sons of God. With the prime vision- Disciples now and apostles ahead.

    - A Holy Ghost University, for teaching and equipping sons with the knowledge and power of the Holy Spirit.

    - A Sanctuary where the whispers of the Holy Spirit intertwine with the eternal truths of God's Word.

2. **Infinity Life Center**: Also called as "The Father's Palace" where the Holy Spirit dwells and the sons of God celebrate life like Heaven on earth.
3. **Agape's House:** A sacred space to flow in deep intimacy

with God.

4. **Passion Prayer Band:** An early morning online prayer group fostering intercession and revival.

Dr. Wesley Abraham's ministry extends to creative outreach initiatives, including co-hosting children's programs on *Angel TV*, organizing *Angel Star Junior* talent shows, and leading corporate prayer groups. His efforts culminated in the establishment of the *Glorious Bikers Club*, combining fellowship and evangelism for biking enthusiasts.

Philanthropy and Global Impact

In 2006, Dr. Wesley Abraham founded the *Pillaigal Charitable Trust*, a registered NGO dedicated to aiding widows, orphans, and the underprivileged. The trust supports life-saving surgeries, provides livelihood tools such as autorickshaws and tricycles, and donates essential items like oxygen cylinders, bedsheets, and food to those in need. His passion for creative ministry also led to the launch of *FM Kondattam*, an online radio station that has reached listeners in over 350 countries with messages of hope and love. From 2007 to 2010, his initiatives, such as *Knight Lamps Tracts* and the *J4US SMS Ministry*, impacted countless lives by drawing them closer to God's love.

Contributions to Worship and Music

As an adorer of the Triune God, Dr. Wesley Abraham has released gospel albums like *Jeevane Jesus* in Jerusalem and *Jayabelamaanavar* in Malaysia, with more projects underway. He has also produced one of the songs from *Jebathotta Jeyageethangal* album. His love for music and worship has been an integral part of his ministry, enriching the worship experience for believers worldwide.

International Ministry

Dr. Wesley Abraham's ministry spans the globe, reaching countries such as Singapore, Malaysia, China, Sri Lanka, Israel, Sweden, France and the U.S. Since 2019, he has been conducting *Holy Spirit Camps* worldwide, bringing transformative encounters to believers. He has also funded church constructions in Sri Lanka and gifted musical instruments to churches.

A Life Rooted in Purpose

Through his ministries and philanthropic work, Dr. Wesley Abraham has become a beacon of hope and a vessel of God's grace, saving lives and leading people to Christ. Above all, he remains a son after God's heart, fully surrendered to His will, and dedicated to glorifying Him in every aspect of his life and ministry. His life's mission is guided by the verse: "As many as are led by the Spirit of God, these are sons of God." Romans 8:14 NKJV. As an anointed man of God, he continues to serve as a devoted spiritual father, visionary leader, and son of the Most High, closely walking with the Spirit of God, inspiring sons to embrace a high standard of life, marked by glory, excellence, and the blessings of elevated purpose, encouraging them to step into their destined greatness.

Foreword

It is both an honor and a privilege to write these words for someone so dear to my heart—my husband. What you hold in your hands, Revelations of Infinity Life, is not just a book; it is a collection of divine quotes that has been given to him by the Holy Spirit. Throughout the years, I've witnessed his deep connection with the Holy spirit, and this book is a true reflection of that sacred bond.

I have seen first-hand, how the Holy Spirit has moved within him, inspiring and empowering him to share the revelation he has received. The words in these pages were not simply written from his mind, but came from a higher place—that are meant to touch hearts and transform. Revelations of Infinity Life is the first of many books that will carry these heavenly messages, and I am in awe of the way the Holy Spirit works through him.

My husband's commitment to following God's will has always been at the heart of his writing, and his humility in sharing these spiritual truths is a testament to his faith. I know that as you read these words, you will feel the same stirring in your spirit that I've witnessed for so long.

This book is just the beginning. I firmly believe that many more divine revelations will flow through him in the years to come. I am filled with excitement to see how the Holy Spirit will continue to guide his pen and how his future works will uplift and inspire others in profound ways.

It has been a true joy to support him in this journey, and I am deeply proud of what he has accomplished. I pray it touches your heart and soul as deeply as it has touched mine.

With all my love and gratitude,

Grace Mercy J

To The Readers,

We thank God for granting us the privilege of gathering these priceless revelations – freshly baked in Heaven and served hot to us.

We take delight in sharing them with you.
It is our fervent prayer that these words ignite your spirit, awaken your purpose, and elevate you to new heights in Him.

Read it, Remember it and Reproduce it.

GRACE

Throughout the coming ages we will be the visible display of the infinite riches of his grace and kindness, which was showered upon us in Jesus Christ. ~ Ephesians 2:7 TPT

So let us come boldly to the throne of our gracious God. There we will receive his mercy, and we will find grace to help us when we need it most. ~ Hebrews 4:16 NLT

Grace

- Grace provides great counsel.
- Give way for Grace to Lead, Life will be lust free.
- Growing in Grace will Get you Greets at the Gates of Glory.
- Life Multi* applies Grace and Peace.
- Grace is the Force.
- Grace is on continuous Growth. Grace always works against the Grave.
- Grace never favors face value.
- A Man with Revelation of Grace and Truth stays in Light not in Law.
- When Grace acts, Heaven approves.
- Lift is like Grace. Efforts to climb the steps are forbidden.
- Grace Lifts and Escalates Glory.
- Grace is the Gateway to Liberty.
- When you are happy to sow in Grace, You will reap in Glory.

- Men mind muscles and wrestles with the Gods Anointed to solve the puzzles of Grace.
- God's killer Grace saves the sinner from death.
- Grace will never offer Sin.
- Grace will never lead you to sin rather it will redeem you back as Son.
- Grace is an instrument to improvise you.
- Grace keeps you concealed and dry.
- Grace keeps us breathing.
- Grace leads the humble.
- Grace abounds where sin abounds.
- Gaze at Grace for Life.
- Obey Grace. Obey Truth. Obey Life and be ye Love.
- Obedience to Grace brings Life. Obedience to men brings condemnation. Obedience to law brings sin. Obedience to sin brings death.
- Grace swallows guilt.
- Grace is the base for greater glory.
- Grace is the Union point.
- The Grace for Noah, got him a New world.
- Grace alone triumphs sin. Jesus is that Grace of God.
- It starts with you. Be it, whatever Grace creates.

- Don't be emotional about the Cross. Be edified and established by the Covenant Christ Concluded at the Cross. Grace Gave His Life For You.
- Grace never curses or cusses. But "Grace Creates".
- Stop Spilling the ill to kill others. Start Spelling the Grace Pills.
- Preach the Gospel. Practise the Grace.
- Grace damages sins' deep images.
- Grace chasers will be sin slaughters.
- Grace always stays ahead of you.
- Grace is the ACE of Heaven.
- Keep walking in His Spirit. Keep moving in Grace.
- Grace Reigns the Law and Ruins the sin.
- Grace can conquer any soul and be gracious enough not to judge any one by their actions.
- Be of good courage that you are on the walk of righteousness through His Grace.
- "Grace on Face" - The unmerited favour of God.
- Be not afraid, you have the grace and faith to overcome this world.
- We are not religious; we are the revealers of God's grace and mercy.
- Grace Empowers, law forbids.
- Grace is complete, law is incomplete and can be debated.
- Grace can never be broken but law can be.

- Grace is Jesus, the King of Heaven and Earth.
- Grace of Jesus is still free and helps us love freely.
- "Victory" - A Testimony of men who dwell on His Grace and Live for His Glory.
- Depression is an expression of frustration. But we need to have "gracepression" to overcome fret.
- Grace and Truth are twins.
- Grace Produces; Faith releases.
- Grace to Gaze the Gospel is called Revelation.
- To have faith, Grace needs to conquer You.
- If you are a grace creature, you will stay to enjoy the blessings of God.
- Grace fetches you. Glory is the one that rises you.
- Grace gives you wisdom.
- Grace is the bundle of gifted thoughts from God gifted for you forever.
- Grace calls and Grace answers.
- Nobody can judge Grace. It can defend for itself.
- Do not showcase your problem as big and make your Grace look small.
- Grace is not something that gives victory to the vanity.
- Let Grace cover all that's yours and May the Grace produce its fruits on all your blessings.
- Grace never agitates.

- Men of this world and their money is temporary. God of this universe and His Grace are forever Infinite and Eternal.
- Choose Grace. Everything else will fall in place.
- Grace keeps us a Son because it works as a Father.
- Grace runs ahead of us, so that we can follow it.
- Grace favors Blessings.
- Those who wait for Grace are called as Sons.
- Don't try to understand Grace. Live in Grace.
- There is no competition for Grace.
- Grace is the root of love. Forgiveness is the fruit of love. Life is the tree of love.
- The Law was Stated to Push me to God. Grace Gushed out to Gather God in Me.
- Grace conceives salvation.
- Grace is the clarity of salvation.
- Grace understands increase.
- Grace has undivided multiplication.
- Grace creature cannot go through debts.
- Grace will give you rest.
- Grace is Spirit which has an energy.
- Grace is free but not cheap.
- Without Grace, you cannot see God.

- You should see whether Grace grows in you and in your Life, only when grace grows in your heart, revelation will also grow.
- No men can generate Grace and Grace can only call upon Grace.
- Grace can only be supplied and governed by Heaven.
- Grace has to be introduced by men; they can't manufacture Grace.
- It's not prayer, it's Grace that keeps one safe.
- Grace will address all your problems because Grace is Jesus Christ.
- Don't reverse the grace. Enjoy the Grace.
- Faith addresses needs. Grace takes care of Life.
- Faith finds the way. Grace gives the way.
- Law is a serial connection; Grace is a parallel connection.
- Grace is addictive, for no men can generate Grace.
- If there is Grace, there is a way.
- Grace never curses, Grace cures.
- Grace never borrows, Grace fruits.
- God doesn't see you as a sinner but a vessel of Grace.
- Grace will not go in poverty.
- Grace will deliver you in a perfect condition.
- Everyone has faith, Grace perfects faith.
- Grace makes you obedient.

- The essence of Grace is much stronger than holiness.
- Grace will never question.
- Grace has a unique gift of travelling into the past.
- Grace is not for gambling; it is for the Kingdom of God.
- Grace has its own time.

***

LOVE

Love is large and incredibly patient. Love is gentle and consistently kind to all. It refuses to be jealous when blessing comes to someone else. Love does not brag about one's achievements nor inflate its own importance. ~ 1 Corinthians 13:4 TPT

We know how much God loves us, and we have put our trust in his love. God is love, and all who live in love live in God, and God lives in them. ~ 1 John 4:16 NLT

Love

- Love is eternal, well essentially internal.
- Love is eternity in infinity.
- Forgive yourself for the haunting past. Move to Love.
- Love, a force from Heaven.
- Love will never Live alone.
- Love never lost its sight.
- He SHED the Blood and said its FINISHED. That's how He loves You.
- Love Him and Lean on Him. You will live Forever.
- Love is full of power to crown you with Life.
- Love is a definite Trust.
- If you take out the Trust from Love, it becomes Rusty Lust.
- Love breaks debt.
- Love is revealed in word and action.
- Miracle is just an exhibition of God's love.
- Love for God grows when the Holy Spirit talks.

- If a person loves you, they will never let you sin.
- Love is the offering.
- Being prophetical and acting prophetical is just naturally supernatural and it brings to you the Love of Father.
- Love covers sin.
- Faith moves you. Faith moves your problem. But Love moves God.
- Rush of the Spirit, gives your Love a Push forward.
- God loves you deeply and warns you sternly for you are not destitute, but His own Sons.
- Move in Spirit. Move in Love. Faith will Follow.
- A Spirit Man should not get excited by seeing the first verse. He should dwell in the power of God and then Destine in the Love of God.
- God's Love for us is irrevocable and unremovable.
- Love is the will of the Father and it never works to ill any other.
- Love is never ashamed.
- Love never shames.
- Love owes no Ego.
- The deeper the Love, the Whisper the speech.
- Love has the power to produce Life.
- Let not the Love hide.
- We Love to see Miracles happen. He Happens to do Miracles for Love.

- Ever knew what's the Best Miracle? It's He in you and you in Him.
- The deeper the Love, the stronger the Faith.
- Never push to Love. Wish to Love.
- The Lord releases Treasures of Love to His Sons.
- Love shall never compel because it's complete.
- Love is the best medicine to heal the world. But most use it as a toxic drug to hurt each other.
- God is Love, preach it well. Preach about your Home, Heaven not Hell.
- How sad! You chose holiness because you fear hell and damnation. Choose to accept Christ proposed Love and He'll make you Holy through His Spirit.
- If you have Love, don't judge. If you are Love, you can't grudge.
- Some fear the relentless Love of the Father, because it's never gonna leave you.
- We are all Sons of God, don't get the spirit of Cain. You are welcome to be the Son of Love. Offer your Love not your hate.
- Love is in Heaven not in Hell. Next time before you kneel just be chill and get healed.
- No one can love you like Christ Jesus. Come to Him. Become Him.
- Smile Jesus Loves You. Keep it for Life miles, nothing will hurt you.
- True respect never comes out of fear. It's out of Love.

ཉ Love is a fruit of the Spirit; you can find it at the feet of Jesus.

ཉ Demanding Love is Demeaning Love.

ཉ If you can't Walk in Love. Better Stay in Love. Love is Prime.

ཉ Keep your Love working in you. For Love is ceaseless.

ཉ Ceaseless prayers and Limitless Love, brings countless Blessings and unspeakable Joy.

ཉ This is PEACE, to know we're Loved and Favoured by the Creator.

ཉ To always be in Love, remember people for their best quality and remind yourselves the help they did to you.

ཉ Life belongs to the Loyal lovers of the Most High.

ཉ Express yourself to those who can afford it in Love.

ཉ Love is not restless, its relentless.

ཉ Love never keeps you idle.

ཉ Our body was provided to do His will with the desire to Love Him and His creation with full heart.

ཉ Love alone can be Holy and that's why the BIBLE is called a Holy book a.k.a Love Book; The only book that speaks of Life for sinners who Love, learning to Love and romance from the chapters of God's own faithfulness.

ཉ Love alone can be Holy and complete.

ཉ If appearance has to do anything with anointing, then I tell you- people, always guess it wrong. Love is complete.

- All things that are beautiful, are not complete but every complete thing is beautiful. Be complete in Love.
- Love is a thankful prayer for the Joy that has been found in a person is missing in the rest. Keep Loving!
- Moving behind a crowd is not a way, Moving the crowd behind you is a new way. Find righteousness and peace will follow you. Believe truth, trust God, Love Life, you will excel in finding a new way.
- We are confident in God's Love and His Son Jesus Christ who gave His Holy Ghost for us to walk in the Way of Glory.
- People Love Jesus because He lives and Loves.
- Sometimes Money and Mind fails Love.
- Lord loves to hear your whispers of thanks and He hates murmurs.
- The fight between Love and Lust is harmful for a soul.
- Settle to Love and owe your Life to peace and glory.
- Love hails Life and lust kills Life.
- Love Returns Life.
- Love is an investment.
- Love never enslaves.
- To Love anyone is every Human's Right. But to be loved is a divine gift.
- When Holy Spirit is working in you, He is 1000% strong and right... Go get the Life of Love.
- Bulldoze the pain with Love.

- Dwell in the Power of God and Destine the Love of God, You'll be the Power House.
- The best Friday - The unchanging act of true Love.
- Men might never understand the deepest Love of God for him, until he opens up for Christ Jesus.
- I admire Human's Love to care, Protect, Possess and Promise Life Long companionship. But I'm awestruck at the Cross of Calvary.
- If you really Love Him, you will sneak your time for Him.
- Love bonds, but never keeps you in bondage.
- A heart to Love God = A heart to Love his own.
- When everything else fades, He still loves you.
- Step in to the Love of Christ and step out as Lovely as Christ. He is waiting for you.
- When God has blessed you, don't dress like the world. Clothe like a Queen, Feast like a King, Ride like a Prince, Be Safe like a Princess, Live like a Lord and Love like a Soldier.
- Love will always step forward.
- If you need to be complete, you have to be in Love and need Love.
- We are not living out of money; we are living out of Love.
- Love is never subjected to Terms and Conditions.
- Love for God grows when Holy Spirit talks.
- Walking in Love is walking in Spirit, but the Love is never carnal.

- Love never demands, it supplies.
- Love never nourishes demands, but fulfills every need with cherish.
- The only call that everyone in Christ makes- 'Come all ye burdened, Christ Jesus loves you and assures you rest in earth and in Heaven.
- Faith is the seed; Love is the fruit.
- Lust cannot kill the Love of God.
- Your Love will ruin the sins of others.
- The best Love is not to think about the next moment.
- Love never sucks your energy, it fills you with energy.
- Being clever and cunning never beats a Love-filled humble heart.
- Prophetic word is the key only if you open with Love.
- Love is the legal transaction in Heaven.
- Depth of His Love is measured by the trust of your Life.
- Love keeps you beautiful. Truth keeps you humble. Spirit keeps you joyful.
- Don't let lust limit the Love.
- Greatest discipline is Love.
- God is love. None can God. He is a gift.
- Temptations has to be threatened by your Love.
- A single word can create a fight if there is no Love.
- You cannot cultivate Love.

- Without Love if you get anything consider it as an expense.
- Love is not sorrow; Love is joy.
- Love should be loud not mild.
- The Bible says that you have only one debt, that is Love.
- Never Love in flesh, Love in Spirit because, God is Love and Spirit.
- He never created us because of need, He created us out of desire and Love.
- God's holiness is Love.
- Love of God will wash you, but the Anointing will warn you.
- Your strength comes from Love.
- Answer for Love in faith is Action.
- Love expressed in action is Faith.
- Miracles happen in Love.
- He opens a reservoir for you to believe in His Love.
- Prayer is a Love letter.
- Every prayer is gonna be a Love story.
- Love invites gifts.
- Faith is Love being solid and Love is being tender.
- His Love makes you Holy.
- When Love is working inside you, power is the payment to you.

- Faith and Love accepts anything which strengthens.
- You have the right to be authoritative, but make sure you are under love.
- God loves your heart not mind.
- Unworthy, fit for nothing and useless can be loved by all worthy.
- If you are in Love, you should carry your lover along with His child.
- Love is a responsibility.
- Devoted lovers will crazily seek Him.
- Worship is distributing His Love to the ones who has not experienced it.
- The greatest beauty is "God loves you".
- If only responsibility exists and no Love, never do it.
- God created us out of love, not because of any need.
- Love doesn't have an end, so it's everlasting.
- From MANGER to the CROSS, the author proclaimed the message of LOVE with the Word called CHRIST JESUS.
- Love has no language, yet it speaks to the heart.
- Love is so full of forgiveness, it should be God.
- Love is so gentle, it should be a man.
- Love is so jealous, definitely, it's a woman.
- Love never leaves us alone, it should be a mother.

- Love never forgets to feed us when we need, it should be a Father.
- Love is so careless, it should be a kid.
- Love is so feasible, it must be a friend.
- Love is so confident, just like a young lover.
- Love is full of expectations, it should be the husband.
- Love is so demanding, it acts as a wife.
- Love is undefeated and that's how it's Eternal.
- Finally Love stays with the undeserved to walk him through Heaven, that's why Love is Christ Jesus. The way, the truth and the Life.

***

LIFE

A fountain of life was in him, for his life is light for all humanity. ~ John 1:4 TPT

And in this fellowship we enjoy the eternal life he promised us. ~ 1 John 2:25 NLT

Life

- Keep your spiritual life higher, so that your personal Life will be Fire.
- The best part of Christian Life is not getting the promise verses but remembering them at time of need.
- Don't betray yourself by self-righteousness and satisfied spiritual Life.
- You are His Life and His reason to be God.
- Honor your offerings with Obedience and Life will follow you forever.
- Don't let the tongue cry for curses because when it cracks with being cold, it swells with curses. So, keep it as a blazing fire for Life.
- Make Jesus the driver and conductor of your Life.
- Jesus is the best partner of your Life.
- Every Way has a Life and is a living thing.
- It all depends on the size of your lips, some lie to die, some confess to Life.
- Heaven is an Avenue with the Tree of Life.

- Being in His Spirit will profit our soul and to yield to it will blossom forth the blessings in our Life.

- Life is so important than Luxury.

- Each passing day is an experience gained; never fret your Life.

- Recruit Giant Killers in your team and not the Giants. Believe Life, you are made to defeat the deaf Giants.

- Bitterness is a jerk. To Live Life abundantly, forgive everyone and carry on your Blessed Life.

- Never feel pity on yourself, it will just drain your aspirations. You may fall, be pushed down, ignored, brutally assaulted, shown wrong directions, face closed doors, put to shame but remember the first thought that aspired you to run and to win. Don't blame the situations, the scenarios or the surroundings. Believe in the Source called LIFE, Move on and speak Life; Victory will be yours, it will never be a selfish act. You are a blessing in this Life.

- Life is made this way with ups and downs almost being a part of our pulse, but remember to hold on, Life is beautiful to live all through your pains and passions.

- The power of Life is in doing good.

- Through pain was this Power of Life restored to many. To break free from sin and death and to, bond Heaven and Earth.

- If you don't affirm your authority on your Life, it will be stupidity.

- Supernatural lifestyle is Simple Truth.

- Life is a crown, don't keep it in a pawn shop.

- Christian Life is a complete, successful and accomplished Life.
- When you allow Jesus to work in your Life it will be whole and complete.
- We are not living an ordinary Life. We are living a prophetical Life.
- Jesus Christ, the Message of Life is much more important than the Miracles of Jesus.
- Prayer is the breath of Life.
- Stand Affirm in the ways of the Spirit, Life will Flow through the Spirit to your Lineage.
- Prayer Life is not shouting. Prayer Life is sensing His presence and speaking in Spirit.
- Bible is not a subject book, it's a Lifeline.
- Active forever state is called Life.
- Life has been created to us.
- God makes Life interesting not questioning.
- Let your testimonies be filled with Truth and Life.
- The voice of the Lord is Life.
- World is behind wealth; God is behind Life.
- Christian Life is not a known living, it is living an unknown Life.
- Life is not awakening, it's always awakened.
- There is no sickness, death and sin in the Life of Jesus.

- When you go to a selfish life from a selfless Life, your Life becomes a source of mockery.
- Untold testimonies suppress blessings in other's Life.
- To minister to God, you need Life (breathe of God-the Holy Spirit).
- Life is a fertile land; you shall reap in plenty of what you sow.
- Destroy the Depth of Doubt. Say Yes to Life.
- Demons Demand Death; Father Favors us with Life.
- Life has answers for every question you have, just have the patience to get it revealed.

***

THE FATHER and KINGDOM

I will be your Father, and you will be my sons and daughters, says the Lord Almighty. ~ 2 Corinthians 6:18 NLT

Go and announce to them that the Kingdom of Heaven is near. ~ Matthew 10:7 NLT

The Father and Kingdom

- You can understand God; but you can't define God.
- God is not a Sunday worker; so, God's temple should not be closed.
- If you don't have the Spirit of God, you have the spirit of story makers.
- Shame comes on people who call all as spiritual father.
- Be vigilant to the spirit that runs to every tent, end of the day, it ruins the Holy Spirit.
- Resist the devil and assist the Kingdom.
- Wisdom is Kingdom property.
- Kingdom mind's never mind dooms day.
- Kingdom is not for the weak but it is for the strong.
- He uses the rubbish and the foolish, to establish His Kingdom.
- Your expenditures should always be with the Kingdom of God.
- Wisdom is for Kingdom.
- To rule is to protect the Kingdom.

- When you know how to multiply for the Kingdom, you will have to become a ruler.
- Don't worry, the Good times are ahead. The enemy will never appreciate it and men will never accept it. Go forward and walk in Spirit, because God cares and it's you He has trusted to Glorify Him. Glory Belongs to God and Kingdom belongs to the Creator.
- Let's build the kingdom of God not our own ministries.
- Heaven is a place for toppers.
- Heaven is not made for beggars, it is made for Kings.
- Church is not a pauper's place; Church is a King's palace.
- Crowds can't bring your crowns, only kings can.
- Fasting makes kings.
- The one who knows to rule isn't a king; the one who is chosen by God is.
- If you constantly listen to His counsel for 365 days, the next one will be a kingly counsel.
- Walking in Spirit leads to Kingship.
- A Christian is not a single person; a Christian is a family of Heaven.
- When you soak yourself in the presence of the Lord, the Heaven will rejoice.
- Heaven is not a public place; heaven is God's place.
- Heaven is in no hurry; heaven has no worry.
- Heaven is a big house, not a military force.

- Heaven gives you liberty, you can also be heaven.
- Your economy should be from Heaven.
- People will use you, but Heaven will purpose you.
- Be Trending in Heaven.
- Someone inside you is so Holy that He will take you to heaven.
- Heavenly wisdom is given to you to have the heavenly riches.
- You are a property of Heaven.
- You are a proper property of Heaven.
- "I"- the stronger the letter, the more respect you get in this world... The humbler it is, the open Heavens will be on its knees to lift you up. Decide and move ahead.
- Heaven is a product-based company not a project-based company.
- You are a tax-free property of Heaven.
- Tithing is made in Heaven.
- We are established, authorized and victorious people sent from heaven.
- We belong to Heavenly management.
- When the world casts you out, the heaven accepts you.
- Honor every manifestation from the Holy Spirit. To be led by the Holy Spirit, you must be yielded to the Holy Spirit, if you yield to the Spirit, you will become Holy Ghost's Heaven.

- When the Heavenly portals open super natural things will happen.
- Heaven is not a dummy place; it's a place where something new happens every second.
- You will not be in compulsion in heaven.
- Its first the glory of God and then God Himself.
- God will not just let the glory shine; He will be your glory.
- Set apart, Step away and Seek Glory.
- It's not a bunch of people you need, all you need is the one right person behind you to walk in glory.
- Implement the Power of I am and you will find the Increase of Glory in you.
- Glory is not man made; it is God driven.
- Pain is temporary; Glory is forever.
- We work for the Government of Heaven.
- We are not after men but after the Kingdom of God.

***

THE KING

Jesus told him, "I am the way, the truth, and the life. No one can come to the Father except through me. ~ John 14:6 NLT

On his robe at his thigh was written this title: King of all kings and Lord of all lords.~ Revelation 19:16 NLT

The King

- Jesus' birth is the Good News and as long as He is alive on the Throne, it's a Good Time.
- The next best person for you is Jesus, He is your Helper.
- Fit into the shoes of Jesus.
- Many treat Jesus like a teacher, only few have Him as the Father.
- Don't fast, only feast when Jesus is with you.
- Jesus never fixes the matches; He makes the matches.
- Jesus is a traveller.
- Devil causes disturbance, Jesus gives us deliverance.
- Jesus could not do anything without the Father. Father instructed Him and instrumented Him.
- If you have the fear of the Lord, your generations will see Jesus.
- If you don't see every one through the Door called Jesus, everyone will be ugly.
- When you know the way you need to travel, Jesus will provide the vehicle you need.

- In the midst of Jesus, miracles happen. Jesus was never in the midst of miracles. Seek Jesus, miracles will work their way.
- With Jesus, Increase is Imminent.
- Small Boat with Jesus can take in large fishes, Try it.
- Jesus was Flawless and made the lawless complete.
- Pharisees could not take Jesus because He was an unprofessional preacher but they forgot to identify that He was the nominated preacher to professionals.
- Jesus was never a miracle machine.
- Genesis was in Jesus.
- Jesus cares for me now, then and forever.
- Jesus is not a half-baked bread. He is a complete bread.
- Jesus did God's will precisely and not randomly.
- Look unto Jesus not Moses. Seek Canaan and not Egypt. Live in Heaven and not in Havoc.
- Power of Jesus is not a mediocre power.
- Jesus feet is the greatest financial wallet.
- Men carry wallet, women carry the feet of Jesus.
- Without Jesus, family is a trap.
- If you want Jesus, you should be led by Jesus.
- Being with Jesus is a miracle.
- Every name under the earth and above the heavens is the reflection of Jesus Christ.

- Excess of care is worrying; the delivery point is Jesus.
- Jesus didn't have an image for Himself, He wanted Father to be His image.
- If you give your tomb to Jesus, you will not have death.
- We don't promote a religion; we promote a Person (Jesus).
- You can do all things except becoming the sacrifice like Christ Jesus.
- When you are in a place where you can imitate Jesus, you will be able to have direct contact with the Father.
- Jesus is a heavenly clock who runs around the Father.
- We build Jesus and not Babel for fame.
- Christ has given everything to us not to rule over Him, but to let Him rule over you.
- Start every day and end everyday with Christ.
- Ignoring Christ inside you is a stage set for Puppets.
- Christ is the Source, not a Resource.
- Remember, Christ is not the Accuser. He is the Saviour.
- Christ is not a religious leader; Christ is the King of Kings.
- Politics has never conquered Christ body.
- Christmas means CareElse.
- The cure for every curse is Christ.
- The pact that you have with Christ will have an impact on your generations.
- The crucified Christ is our cure.

- You are insulated by Christ not isolated by Corona.
- Aspire to be the credibility than a celebrity for Christ.
- Imitate the Intimate Christ.
- Preach the resurrected Christ and not your ruined mind.
- A Happy Family is not where everyone is a Christian, but is Christ Like.
- Go with the Resurrected Christ than the Researched Christ.
- Christ is the living Bridegroom. If you don't live for Him or according to His command then it is prostitution.
- Never blame others for failing to come near Christ. The invitation was for you.
- Christ can only grow and press on, but not backslide or subside.
- When Christ lives in you there is nothing called impossible. It's only Supernatural.
- When Christ grows inside you, you will become a respectable person.
- Live as Christ else whatever you do will be evil.
- Christ has never lost the hope you had on Him. He is a conqueror and He lives in Victory.
- You cannot define Christ; you should explore Him.
- Christ is a nurse not a curse.
- Don't compromise yourself from being Christ.
- Conversations didn't pull Christ, Christ entered the conversation.

THE SPIRIT

But He was wounded for our transgressions, He was bruised for our iniquities; The chastisement for our peace was upon Him, And by His stripes we are healed. ~ Isaiah 53:5 NKJV

You must understand this at the outset: Interpretation of scriptural prophecy requires the Holy Spirit, for it does not originate from someone's own imagination. No true prophecy comes from human initiative but is inspired by the moving of the Holy Spirit upon those who spoke the message that came from God. ~ 2 Peter 1:20,21 TPT

The Spirit

- Consistently listen to constantly flow in Spirit.
- Let your body be soaked in Spirit.
- Waiting on God keeps your Spirit awake.
- Be patient to know who the Spirit of God is.
- Never deny, nor annoy the Holy Spirit.
- If you want to reap the fruits of the Spirit, stop judging.
- Be renewed in the spirit of your mind.
- Flowing in Spirit will keep you glowing in spirit.
- When you are humble and keep yourself low, the Holy Spirit will flow.
- When there is the presence of Holy Spirit, there is deliverance.
- Assist the Holy Spirit; do not resist the Holy Spirit.
- Go deeper in Spirit and stronger in fellowship.
- If you do it in spirit, expect in spirit.
- God can fill you with the Holy Spirit, but you can refill you with your own spirit.

- A confused spirit is many spirits acting at the same time.
- You should know the Holy Spirit to know which spirit speaks.
- The world doesn't determine who you are, your spirit does.
- It's contagious for a righteous man to be in spirit.
- A man is just a clay, if he doesn't have Holy Spirit.
- Assist the Holy Spirit and you will have freedom.
- You can't have the skip button for the Holy Spirit.
- Don't restrict the Holy Spirit.
- Intensify the intimacy with Christ. For more information, call on the Holy Spirit.
- Revival is receiving from the Holy Spirit round the clock.
- Holy Spirit will see the depth in you.
- Holy Spirit will not let you to obey negativity.
- Jesus is the funnel and through it the Holy Spirit is poured inside you.
- Holy Ghost doesn't confuse you.
- If you don't defy your fleshy thoughts, you will never grow in Spirit.
- Ministry is not from men but from Holy Spirit.
- Holy Spirit is the gentlest person in the Trinity.
- Holy Spirit's instructions are for Supernatural investments.
- Keep yourself free from imagination when you invite the Holy Spirit.

- The everyday epistles of His Spirit are delivered to you. Spread it within you and around you.
- The dominance of your flesh and others would decrease the increase of the Holy Spirit.
- Familiarity of the Holy Spirit will make you a family with the Trinity.
- Holy Spirit is a great caretaker.
- Acknowledge the Holy Spirit because it's a one to one conversation between you and the Holy Spirit.
- Holy Spirit is the best Match Maker. He Chose you for Christ.
- Holy Spirit will never irritate you but irrigate you.
- Holy Spirit seasons are for resurrected reasons.
- When you invite the Holy Spirit, He is sure to search your heart and hear the soul's cry.
- Holy Spirit proclaims the power of patience and tolerance not arrogance.
- Holy Spirit never brings mutiny, He is for unity.
- To Experience Heaven, allow your mind to tune with your spirit. and when your spirit, adheres to the Holy Spirit, you are now in Heaven.
- If you don't walk and believe in Spirit, you are making Jesus Christ as an empty vessel.
- Greatest teacher is the Holy Spirit and He will make sure that you are the best in class.
- For person who knows Christ knows the Holy Spirit.

- Holy Spirit does not come in pressure.
- Holy Spirit is precious. Don't defame Him.
- Holy Spirit is not short lived.
- When the Spirit of God is in you, you will not be an ordinary person you will be an exalted person.
- Holy Spirit never shows off, He only shows up.
- Holy Spirit is a living personality.
- The Holy Spirit says Receive the power of God and Release the power of God.
- Don't let the Holy Spirit become dormant in you.
- Spirit of the Lord is not a barking dog but a LION.
- Holy Spirit never makes you think, but makes you discern.
- Holy Spirit is the starting and finishing point.
- Holy Spirit never gossips.
- Don't be responsible to the world, be responding to the Holy Spirit.
- Holy Spirit is never an agitator. He is the comforter.
- Holy Spirit is our companion. He is not a one-day beautician.
- Holy Spirit is the rushing wind.
- Wisdom is from Holy Spirit.
- Holy Spirit will not attract you. He will turn your attention towards The Father.

- God is God, Holy Spirit is Holy Spirit and Jesus Christ is the super Saviour.
- The relationship between Mary and Jesus is Holy Spirit.
- Holy Spirit is one, it doesn't mean that you have to be like one another.
- Holy Spirit is found in any form.
- Holy Spirit is not a broken chain, He is a continuous chain.
- Christ replaced Himself with the Holy Spirit.
- Spirit is a fire.
- Power of Holy Spirit will never ask permission.
- Holy Spirit entertains and edifies.
- Nothing will start new until it is inspired by the Holy Spirit.
- Have the Spirit of Christ to create from where there is nothing.
- Jesus is universal guidance; Holy Spirit is parental guidance.
- Accuser is ready to travel; only the Holy Spirit, your defender will always be with you.
- Holy Spirit prepares you for the groom.
- Holy Spirit gives inheritance of everything not just the outline.
- Holy Spirit is seeking an imperfect body with a perfect heart.
- If you are filled with the Holy Spirit, you are filled with the power of God as well.

Never suppress Holy Spirit and impress people.

ANOINTING

But the wonderful anointing you have received from God is so much greater than their deception and now lives in you. There's no need for anyone to keep teaching you. His anointing teaches you all that you need to know, for it will lead you into truth, not a counterfeit. So just as the anointing has taught you, remain in him. ~ *1 John 2:27* TPT

You prepare a feast for me in the presence of my enemies. You honor me by anointing my head with oil. My cup overflows with blessings. ~ *Psalms 23:5* NLT

Anointing

- Anointing is a responsibility.
- Anointing is an authority.
- Anointing never lies.
- Give power to the Spirit, that's the anointing.
- Anointing is not a profile for a servant, it is a personal relationship with the Father.
- Let your Anointing flow to keep you away from the enemy's claws.
- Anointing never brags arrogance.
- Anointing is not the super power delivered to anyone. It is the power to the chosen to Conquer fear and doubts, to inherit the throne and crown that Lord Jesus has ordained.
- Anointing will never leave you orphan.
- Receive the anointing one more time to renew your strength on the way to success.
- Anointing should come from Spiritual presence, not from physical presence.
- Anointing is to develop your attitude and build the Kingdom of God.

- Anointing inside you will not blame anyone.
- Lord's anointing will give you Victory, Glory and Prosperity.
- Anointing is not for sale, but it's very much available for everyone in Christ.
- Honour the anointing. Harvest the Abundance. Abigail honoured the Anointing on David and that anointing took her to be the bride.
- Anointing is not spoken to your ears; it's spoken to your calling.
- Anointing is a profile for you to fill.
- Don't annoy your anointing.
- Embrace your anointing.
- Anointing is not a subject.
- Anointing never expects your experience.
- Anointing never dies, it grows.
- Fear and respect the anointing.
- No common man can speak about anointing.
- Anointing is a teacher.
- Don't abandon the anointing and lose the abundant Life.
- Anointing is not a culprit, anointing is Christ.
- Anointing will fill you.
- Anointing is not a pride, it's a treasure.
- Anointing will not make anyone lazy.

- Be Remarkably addicted to the new wine called anointing.
- Anointing can't be self-used.
- Anointing is for the gospel; you will benefit when other people enjoy out of it.
- Anointing is not man made, it's of God.
- Anointing cannot be forced, a forced anointing leads to frustration.
- Don't get the anointing fit and lose it, let the anointing flow.
- When you are submitted under the anointing, you can't add ifs and buts to it.
- Anointing is the process called breaking the yokes.
- Anointing is that act of pressure on the bondage.
- Anointing breaks the yoke not your neck.
- Anointing defines(teaches) me to me.
- Don't handle the anointing, let the anointing handle you.
- Enact the anointing, you are not just a receiver of anointing but a transmitter of anointing.
- Your Anointing is not a barking dog. It's a roaring lion.
- Anointing is multi-currency both of heaven's and world's.
- Anointing is for you to show Christ as the King.
- Anointing is not a dress, it's a breath.
- Anointing will warn you.

- Anointing is not to do your will; anointing is to do God's will.
- Anointing speaks to us what the Father has been teaching us.
- Anointing of sons will not criticize the Father.
- Anointing is your lover, don't defeat Him.
- Do not compare your anointing.
- Anointing is an answer; not a question.
- Kingship is anointing.
- Anointing is not cheap; anointing is costly.
- Anointing is the teacher.
- Anointing is not a game; anointing is a throne.
- Don't take what your anointing hasn't taught you.
- Anointing is never hasty.
- Don't control the anointing, allow the anointing to teach you.
- Your anointing is priceless.
- Anointing is needed although your Life.
- Anointing should and will run parallelly.
- Anointing is like a Tsunami which has come to change the whole place.
- Anointing is against anything that tempts you and doesn't treat you well.
- Anointing will make you new everyday.

- Anointed are not a distraction but direction in your Life.
- Anointing will lead you to the captives.
- Voice of the anointed will bring back lives to God.
- Anointing is good conscience.
- Don't expect men to respect the anointing, it's too much for them to understand.
- All who received the Holy Spirit defended their anointing through signs and miracles.
- Anointing should revere anointing.
- If you have received the anointing something supernatural is always around you.
- Don't make the anointing judgmental.
- Anointed can't lament, for His anointing will break every yoke.
- You are unteachable when you go back to the same person who didn't respect your anointing.
- Love anointing connects spiritual father and sons.
- Anointing is the connecting power point to heaven.
- Anointing opens your heart to God.
- Anointing does the work of God in you.
- Anointing doesn't work on murmurs.
- Murmuring and grumbling will never prosper anointing.
- God will not anoint a person without a reason.

- If the anointed are not authoritative, who else would be His Spirit will make you perfectly humbled to reign over the earth...
- Have a Humble attitude before the God's anointed. Live in Spirit to know What i have quoted.
- An anointed cannot speak `n' number of words... An anointed can only speak God numbered words.
- Your calling and anointing should remind you about Jesus.
- Holy Spirit will never take appreciation from the unanointed.
- You should be God's anointed not men's appointed.
- When anointed speaks, they speak heaven to you.
- God never keeps His anointed with Him, He sends them to give.
- Anointing is attractive, you should love the one who anointed you.

***

FAITH

You have all become true children of God by faith in Jesus Christ! ~ Galatians 3:26 TPT

For we live by faith, not by what we see with our eyes. ~ 2 Corinthians 5:7 TPT

Faith

- Faith Fires the Future.
- Let your words be filled with motivation and not empty emotions. Send out each word to spread the Truth. Fill your words with Life and seed them because the season is due for the faith to raise in favor.
- Power of faith is to lose yourself to your divine destiny.
- Faith is contagious. Speak victory when you lead and when you stand alone because you are part of God's plan.
- Don't project your fears, project your faith.
- If you abide by your thoughts you'll lose. If you abide by thoughts of God, you are a champion of faith.
- Faith is never childless.
- Faith is productive.
- Faith will always listen to what the deliverance says.
- Faith is something built upon the Word of God for His purpose.
- God does not demean your faith.
- Faith can't be manufactured, it is inborn.

- Multiply faith and resist doubts.
- Your faith system works with Words, words that you speak, words that you hear.
- Faith has no feelings.
- Gospel is the source of salvation. Words of faith strengthens us to experience the promises in salvation.
- Faith is a continuous focus.
- Faith is Spirit sent by the Father in Heaven.
- To experience his compassion and mercy you need faith.
- Faith starts with hearing and ends with speaking.
- Faith elevates whereas fear demotes.
- Don't let Gods faith lead to dustbins. Take your doubts to dustbins.
- Faith is not an act. It's a relationship.
- Faith comes by submission.
- Faith is not a definition; faith is God Himself.
- Faith brings God to live.
- It's not common faith, you should have a supernatural faith which shows you unique.
- If your faith is not increasing, it means it's decreasing.
- Anything that comes by faith is Holy.
- An energetic spirit create faith.
- Faith is the greatest miracle.

- Faith Acts.
- Miracle without Faith and Truth is just magic and vanity.
- Supernatural without Faith and Truth is just vanity.
- A stone of Faith in a sling of praise that can kill Goliaths.
- Author of faith is JESUS.
- Fear is negative faith.
- Faith is higher level.
- Faith is a resurrected thing.
- Your faith level is your finance.
- Being self-sufficient is a lazy faith.
- Faith can't be impotent, faith is a warehouse, a production unit.
- Faith is for everything, not for one thing.
- Doubt is from devil, faith is from the Father.
- Your measurement of faith is Christ.
- Faith assurance is the Holy Spirit.
- Faith is not making things happen; Faith is seeing things happen.
- Fear stops Holy Spirit to work and doubt stops faith.
- Faith trains the physical body to run with the spiritual body.
- You lacking faith is dishonoring God.
- You don't need a faith system, you need a manufacturing

faith system.

- When you wanna have faith, shut your mouth until faith fills you.
- Faith increases only for those who wait.
- For His strength to be manifested in you, you need faith.
- Faith is a way of living.
- Live with the thoughts of faith in your prosperous future.
- Faith fades out when you fail to remember His favors.
- Mustard Faith, Moves Fearful Mountains.
- It's not "Easy", it never was, until you reap the fruits of your "Faith".
- Faith never postpones.
- Faith is immediate.
- Faith is a Fruit when you act on His Words. Faith is a Gift when you act and He favours it with the word.
- The threat to faith starts from tolerating fear.
- Spiritual Life is exercising faith by continuous hearing of Word of God.
- Faith is now. Hope is the next moment of Faith.
- Faith is a Gift! Faith is a Fruit! So, gift the fruit of the Spirit to the Father of the Spirit.
- Faith Fades out when you forget His favours.

***

HEALING and PROPHECY

But He was wounded for our transgressions, He was bruised for our iniquities; The chastisement for our peace was upon Him, And by His stripes we are healed. ~ Isaiah 53:5 NKJV

You must understand this at the outset: Interpretation of scriptural prophecy requires the Holy Spirit, for it does not originate from someone's own imagination. No true prophecy comes from human initiative but is inspired by the moving of the Holy Spirit upon those who spoke the message that came from God. ~ 2 Peter 1:20,21 TPT

Healing and Prophecy

- Jesus never Hurts, He Heals.
- Jesus is a Good Samaritan who heals your wounds.
- Togetherness is a great healer to the kingdom of God.
- You are the Healing Not a Hurt.
- Be the Heal, Be the Help. Be what He needs you to Be.
- Your word should heal people and help people.
- We need our bodies to be healthy for Spirit of God to work in full force. Without the body, spirit can do nothing. Jesus is sitting at the right hand of God with His own body. We are a spirit being living in a body with a soul.
- Let every portion of yours live in healing.
- Healing is promotional. Promote your health.
- Resurrection is healing.
- No healing is greater than the shoulder of Jesus.
- Lazy people cannot be a prophet; lazy people cannot be an apostle.
- Every act of a prophet is a prophecy.

- Apostles is to do what God says for others; Prophet is to do what God says.
- Every prophecy is as good as your name.
- We don't force prophecy, we foresee prophecy.
- Don't use prophecy without decency.
- Being a prophet, if you are watching a vision of a lustful person, it is equal to watching pornography.
- Prophecy for everyone is LIFE and not LIE.
- The prophecy spoken on you wants you to be alive. Be available for it to take its course.
- Prophet is not an entertainer. Prophet is an Eternal trainer. You can't go to a prophet for your profit.
- Prophets and preachers cannot be in the same place. They have to move to places where God tells.
- A Prophet is not a hotspot for you to connect to God. He is the spotlight of God's heart.
- Testimony can become prophecy. Be the testimony.
- Prophecy is a word of encouragement to fulfill your destiny.
- You have a certain time to cancel the wrong word uttered. Every word of a prophet count.
- A prophet is always a profit.
- Prophecy is a bridge built between you and God.
- Prophecy should deliver people and not embarrass them.
- Prophecy should not trouble you but train you.

- A prophet is God's trumpet and never a person's puppet.
- Every act of a prophet is a prophecy.
- Being Good is not a choice but a gifted character.
- Gifts are from God to man; Service is from man to God.
- Salvation is just not another gift. It is the GIFT.
- The body is a gift to carry God and His presence. Your spirit needs one.
- Tongues makes devil trembles.
- Tongues should not be a labor but a favor.
- When you speak in tongues, you speak to highly dignified king with a language of highly dignified kingdom.
- Tongues should elevate thanks.
- Be in Spirit. Speak in tongues. Release the offerings.
- Vision keeps us on, advance and proceed towards the vision.
- A visionless person is blind.
- Miracles are free.
- Miracles never get old, walk beside your miracle.
- The strength of the miracles are in silence.
- The beauty of the miracle is He Himself.
- Miracles are never made from machines.
- You can't force a miracle into someone.

***

PEACE and PROSPERITY

True enrichment comes from the blessing of the Lord, with rest and contentment in knowing that it all comes from him. ~ *Proverbs 10:22 TPT*

Don't worry about anything; instead, pray about everything. Tell God what you need, and thank him for all he has done. Then you will experience God's peace, which exceeds anything we can understand. His peace will guard your hearts and minds as you live in Christ Jesus. ~ *Philippians 4:6,7 NLT*

Peace and Prosperity

- Peace was never man-made.
- Prayer is for you to experience, experience the peace of God.
- A man with full of peace is the greatest miracle.
- Don't miss your peace by investigating.
- Peace in your body is Health; Peace in your soul is Life; Peace in your Spirit is Joy.
- Procrastination to act on the Spirit leads to Peace-less destination.
- Peace cannot be stagnant; it can be transferred to people.
- In Jesus, we have peace at every place.
- Inspire and motivate others to be the best, the peace in your soul is divine and let it overflow, you're called for abundance.
- Peace with yourself is a great battle settled without much sacrifice.
- Rest, relax, refresh, renew, revive. Be in Spirit. Be in Supernatural.
- Investing is an attitude of resting.

- God will give you rest but He will not make you lazy.
- God gives you rest, because He sees the glory in rest in you.
- Holy Spirit is the resting place.
- Rest from stress else you will lose your tress.
- Stress is finding rest when you just missed it at the start.
- The resurrected redeemer is our Rest.
- Rest not Resist the Holy Spirit.
- Come out of your comfort and rest in supernatural.
- Be free to be a fire; Be calm to be a healing balm.
- Prosperity is responsibility; if you fail to be responsible, you intend to be in poverty.
- Remember to repent and reconcile before the pestilence strikes you. If a stern warning word still keeps you cold, danger is at the doors. In the contrary, if it is the word of peace and prosperity, be sure to be in humility and holiness and let the word exalt you.
- Keep away from foul mouths and you shall have peace and prosperity.
- Give way for the Heavenly peace and prosperity to reach you.
- Seed not in pity; seed in prosperity.
- You are a prosperous property of Heaven.
- That thirty dirty silver coins could never see Judas prosper.
- Prosperity is not what men perceives; it's what men receive from Above.

- Prosperity is the Responsibility to feed the needed.
- Prosperity comes when you are under the Anointed Word of Power.
- Walk in Peace for it is prosperity.
- The Word gives prosperity and power.
- Be in peace with the prosperity, you shall then inherit the Heavenly.
- Father's presence is prosperity.
- Prosperity comes when healing happens.
- Don't go for prosperity; you are the prosperity.
- The first principle to prosperity is to give Him the first portion.
- Heaven is a greatest place of economic prosperity.
- Kingdom of God does appreciate prosperity.
- God's beloveds will definitely prosper.
- To be prosperous Praise! Praise! Praise!
- Whatever you do will prosper if the Kingdom is in you.
- Prosperity has ears.
- Enemy wants you to become prosperous because he wants to hunt you down.
- You should be a symbol of prosperity.
- Joy and prosperity are connected; love and prosperity are connected.
- The first principle to prosperity is placing God first.

- Filling up your hearts with thanks will bring prosperity.
- Prosperity comes to a person who praises God.
- God is not a god of Conception. He is a God of Provision.
- Debt is not a personal loan; it's a generational loan.
- Disobedience delivers the debt in dues.
- Obedience Obsoletes Debts.
- Be bold to unfold the gold God gave in you.
- Holy is gold; holiness is pure gold.
- Malls are not glorious riches; His glory is glorious riches.

***

WISDOM

Fear of the Lord is the foundation of wisdom. Knowledge of the Holy One results in good judgment. ~ Proverbs 9:10 NLT

And if anyone longs to be wise, ask God for wisdom and he will give it! He won't see your lack of wisdom as an opportunity to scold you over your failures but he will overwhelm your failures with his generous grace. ~ James (Jacob) 1:5 TPT

Wisdom

- Big idiots are the ones that lose great ideas for small minds.
- Grumblers get priority seat at the gates of groaning.
- Old covenant needs your part of flesh. New Covenant provides His part of flesh.
- Enemy's lies are invisible, but not invincible.
- Don't let darkness creep your mind.
- Keep the ears open for the Lord's voice.
- Giving a fitting reply doesn't make anyone right. It's the answer the world needs. Be the answer not a reply.
- Devil is still a big-time liar. You know it when God Answers Him not.
- Favor is free, don't deny it for any.
- Deep down, everyone appreciates favor, but the difficulty is to accept it when it's for the other person.
- Devil promises what God had already purposed for you. Beware! Realize God.
- Memories bring stories alive in moments, people will value the product. God will value the person.

- Expectation is weakness.
- Your obsessions make you ill.
- Satan can't evaluate your paper; he can only make you miss the exam.
- Darkness has an attitude called doubt.
- Darkness will always have fear and will make you blind.
- God wants us to be Him and men wants us to be them.
- His feet are not failures.
- There is no speed breaker for flight.
- Time, season and space belongs to God.

***

BLESSING

I will make you into a great nation. I will bless you and make you famous, and you will be a blessing to others. ~ Genesis 12:2 NLT

Every spiritual blessing in the heavenly realm has already been lavished upon us as a love gift from our wonderful heavenly Father, the Father of our Lord Jesus—all because he sees us wrapped into Christ. This is why we celebrate him with all our hearts! ~ Ephesians 1:3 TPT

Blessings

- Don't let your blessings to change you and define you, you should define your blessings.
- Your blessings should breed.
- When you swim across your blessings, you will feel frustrated. Try sailing across with the Shepherd, your blessings will bless you.
- The power of your blessings will run through and if you play with it, it will breakthrough.
- Seek the blessings in heaven and it will be given to you.
- Don't force yourself for the blessings of the Lord, Foresee your blessings.
- Don't boast about your blessings.
- Nothing will hurt when God blesses us.
- Never keep the blessing between you and God.
- Every blessing has a name.
- When God blesses you, He protects you.
- If you want blessings, just sing.
- Let your blessing bounce back to you.

- Melchizedek blessings bring the promises out of you.
- When you willingly obey God, He will beneficially bless you.
- Come out of the crowd that wants you to prove. Come to the Father with your heart and be blessed. He will give you all your heart's desires and you will know what belongs to you.
- Blessings cannot be demanded; it will happen in the background.
- Blessings means protection.
- Offering is the result of the blessing; sacrifice is the submission of the blessing.
- No men can desire more than His destined blessings.
- Humble never tumble though they stumble and rumble they will stand as a sample of blessing.
- Heaven's blessings are intentional.
- To bless Jacob, Isaac has to be blind. #Blind Blessings#
- Your work is to expect and the Father's work is to bless you.
- Protection is part of the blessing and that part belongs to God.
- You are not here to miss the blessings but hit the blessings.
- Prayers can alone bring down blessings.
- Boast your blessings to the right person.
- Don't wrestle with your blessings. Let it dwell on you.

- Pursue God as a Master of your blessings.
- When you are in the presence of the Lord, you bring the blessings of the world.
- Blessings should not take you out of your balance.
- There is nothing called easy blessings, it's essay of blessings.
- Heaven is a place where blessing starts.
- When you want to reach the world share the experience, before that, share the blessings.
- Don't lose yourself in the blessing; blessings should be drowned in you.
- Be a blesser than a stresser.
- Jesus is the dispersal of God's blessings.
- God's blessings is a strike not a stroke.
- Blessing is secondary; presence of God is primary.
- Don't rush your blessing; don't push your blessing; God should press your blessings.
- To bless is God's intention, to steal is devil's intention.
- You are the literature of blessings.
- Instant miracles are for everlasting blessings.
- Every blessing is abbreviated in your name.
- Satan uses you as a commodity but God uses you as a blessing.
- Blessing is not milk sucked out of a mother; it should flow from Him.

- It's not about materialistic blessing but wholesome blessings.
- You are blessed because God is good and has set very low standards for you.
- Every miracle in the Bible is for an economic blessing.
- If you win your lust, your brother will be blessed as a witness.
- God creates various planets and directs them to bless you.
- Money matters, follow the Master's money, you will become the Masters of Money.
- Money is just a number and God adds value to it.
- Make the money mind its business, you be the man God made you to be.
- Making money is not a Minister's job, representing the Kingdom does it.
- Money doesn't come only when you sell the land, it comes when you obey.
- Money is my many testimony.
- Caesars are money printers; Christ owns it all.

***

REVELATIONS

I received my message from no human source, and no one taught me. Instead, I received it by direct revelation from Jesus Christ. ~ *Galatians 1:12 NLT*

But when the truth-giving Spirit comes, he will unveil the reality of every truth within you. He won't speak on his own, but only what he hears from the Father, and he will reveal prophetically to you what is to come. ~ *John 16:13 TPT*

For this wonderful mystery, which I briefly described, was given to me by divine revelation, so that whenever you read it you will be able to understand my revelation and insight into the secret mystery of the Messiah. ~ *Ephesians 3:3-4 TPT*

Revelation

- Revelation is God's heart.
- Revelation is not knowledge based, its love based.
- Revelation is Elevation. Relive it every moment.
- If you don't have the revelations which is light anyone can deceive you.
- Revelation is the power in the word.
- Every revelation is a prompt paid cheque. Get paid for giving yourself to the Word of Christ.
- Nothing is revelation until it happens.
- Revelation directs towards glory.
- Revelation is incremental.
- Revelation is not for debate but for experience.
- Revelation gives you a surety.
- Christ revelations comes from intimacy.
- Revelations reverb around you to release overflowing provisions of Heaven.
- Only the revelation can keep the relation alive.

- Revelation is birth.
- Never revolt against your revelations.
- Revelations will resurrect your actions.
- Revelations is never a virtual fantasy, it's the real way to intimacy.
- We make the Gospel complete.
- When you involve Jesus, He will give you the Gospel and make you preach.
- Gospel starts when gossip ends.
- Money doesn't make a person rich; it is the gospel within them.
- Gird like a man, don't gossip around about the Gospel. Gallop with the Gospel.
- The zeal about the gospel comes from the seal of the Holy Spirit.
- Don't let the mystery of gospel diluted by men's story.
- Gospel is all powerful. The problem with the youngster is they seek the Lord and the Word only when there is an obvious need and the rest read the Word of God as daily devotion. But to see the power of the Gospel and its mighty works, one should submit and succeed in loosing entirely to the Spirit of God. He will guide you through the scriptures in alignment with the holy will. Don't try to chase away darkness. Step out, Seek the light and the darkness will flee. Choose light and the rest is miracle.
- Gospel is "free" but not cheap.

- Gospel is so simple that the wise fail and the fools get through.
- Gospel should release people but not bind people.
- Gospel is the complete dictionary of all the Good Words of God.
- Gospel is a gift.
- Gospel is not a dead end.
- Gospel alone can feed salvation and add power.
- Gospel never dies.
- Holy Spirit will take you to delve into scriptures.
- Scriptures are like loan settlements; you will be asked to pay what is possible.
- Whatever the Holy Spirit speaks, the Scripture reveals.
- You can never become beggar when you are reading Scriptures.
- When you have the Spirit of God, you will have the Scriptures of God.
- Not everything that Jesus spoke was in the Scripture, whatever He spoke was a Scripture.
- When you have the Spirit of God, you will have the Scriptures of God.
- You are not a scene in a theater, you are Scripture to live them.
- You can come closer than the Scripture through Spirit.
- Word is not for mind, it's for body.

- The Word can be resurrected only by the Holy Spirit.
- You are not the verse in the calendar but the spoken Word of God.
- God's Word is a working word.
- The knowledge about His word will keep you in abundance.
- You should know the worth of you for you have His word in your mouth.
- Light comes first, then the air and then the Word.
- God is not a robotic God; He speaks new words.
- Every heart has an ear to hear the Word of God.
- Word should visit us.
- The Father of Covenants will not break His Words or turn away from them. It is us who forgot why the Word was provided to us and where we are standing on His promises.
- Mute your mind and open your spirit to flow with His words.
- Being obedient to His Words will keep us awake for His plans and purposes.
- When the Word of God comes to you, even the doughtiest situation can turn into a luxurious one.
- The difference between you and a normal Christian is the Word.
- His Word is uncorrupted and uncompromised.
- Devotion to the Word and submission to the Spirit will work wonders to your soul.

- Don't let the world corrupt your word.
- WORLD = WORD+LORD. Place the LORD before your WORD and YOU will Conquer this WORLD.
- Share the Word when the Word proceeds the work begins and gets established.
- You are the Golden Word of God.
- Fill your world with the Word of the God.
- Receiving a prophetic word is a gift, but to be the prophecy is glory.
- You are what the Word says.
- A picture can convey many things but a word can convey so many blessings.
- If you are a Word of God, you will not be empty, but you will be useful vessels.
- You cannot do or overdo the Word of God.
- Word of God has an address.
- You don't need huge audience to deliver awesome messages; you just need beautiful chosen souls to sit with you to listen to THE WORD.
- When you place God's Verses versus virus; Word will win the world.
- No good news has bad words in it.
- His word is superior than your time.
- Obey the Word of God.
- Holy Spirit is the one-word answer and the word is yes.

- You are not a speaker of the world; you are a speaker of the Word.
- Word of God is not to console you but to change you into a new creation.
- You are born of an uncorrupted word.
- Don't dilute the Word, give it as concentrated as it is.
- There is power in the middle of the Word and Spirit.
- Be consistently under the Word and under the Spirit.
- When the Word keeps working, it will start to become Holy Word.
- Hard Truth exposed. Not to shame you but to let you shine for Him.
- You can take a long way to know the truth but don't get into a wrong way.
- Every heart has an ear to hear the truth.
- Let not the thoughts weigh more than the truth.
- Truth is stronger than you think.
- Truth is knowing you and your God who dwells in you.
- Direct the truth to your heart.
- Holy Spirit is not an information giver, He is a truth speaker.
- Be attentive to the Father's Spirit who lets you walk in Light and Truth, stay away from FEAR.
- Let the Spirit of the Lord lead you in all truth (green pastures).

- The call of truth needs to be answered always, else the lie shall keep you complaining always.
- Be a truthful transaction.
- Roaring truth and loving spirit underline a Christian walk.
- Glory is sufficient for truth.
- Truth is being breathed because you and I are living.
- Truth protected Paul but popularity tried to kill him.
- Truth is not costly; it will set you free so it's not cheap either.
- Root on the Truth.
- The Spirit of Truth will never admit lies as fact.
- Lies always tastes better than the truth, but lies keeps you sick.
- Truth sets you free and lets you know what access you have.
- Heaven is a place where truth breathes. Earth is a place where truth breeds.
- Holy Spirit is not a subject to be taken in class, He is the Truth.
- Respect everyone who knew the truth about themselves.
- Truth will never die, but lie will die.
- Bible is the Holy Spirit driven book.

- Bible is not a hiding place for a treacherous man, it is a hiding place for a loving man.

- Bible is inspired and written by the help of the Holy Ghost. So, Am I.
- Christians read your bible rather than trying to please friends, as it profits your soul and others.
- Bible is not a text to preach, it is a subject line to live.
- Bible is not a subject book, it's a book of mysteries.
- Bible can never be created nor be destroyed.

***

SONSHIP

For as many as are led by the Spirit of God, these are sons of God. ~ *Romans 8:14 NKJV*

And because we are his children, God has sent the Spirit of his Son into our hearts, prompting us to call out, "Abba, Father." ~ *Galatians 4:6 NLT*

Sonship

- Christmas gave us a reason for eternal season to be the Son.
- Son of God should become a God one day.
- We are not here to be the best preacher, pastor or apostle, we are here to be the Son of God.
- Holy Spirit is from the Father and is the Son's greatest treasure which is poured unto us as a covenant for His sacrifice on the cross.
- The Son in the Prison is setting free every Per sons from the Prisons.
- You can't pick the Sons from the crowd, they grow within (inside) you.
- Drought is not for Daddy's Darling Son. Famine is not for the Father's Favorite Son.
- The Son shames the Father when He exalts His fellowship with the Father rather than the relationship.
- Swallow the Sin and follow the Son.
- Prisons aren't for Sons.
- Zion is for Sons.

- Don't paint yourself as saint. Follow the Father, be the Son.
- Death has no power on us, we are "Christsons".
- Saints don't see the sin in everything, they see Son of God in every scene.
- God doesn't ask us all to be like saints but to be like His Son (Jesus), who obeyed God and acted upon His will. To be a son we need to keep away sin.
- Men may come, men may go. But Son of man stays forever at the throne.
- Worries belongs to pigs; Peace belongs to Sons.
- Prophets are the Sons of God delivering the Words of God.
- You can never give any reasons in any seasons to the Sons.
- Don't tell reason to The Son.
- Moses is the man of God; Jesus is the Son of God.
- If you are a son of God, you are Christ.
- We need a son to replicate God.
- Until you have sonship, you cannot be a good brother.
- To have sonship, you need the Spirit of God.
- Sons don't lament on lack and don't lavish in abundance.
- Sons of God are not slaves of any.
- Sons are not invited, they are sent.
- Prison can never imprison Sons.
- We are not saints; we are Sons of God.

- Don't be inspired by men of the world but the Sons of God.
- Paul didn't bring out saints but Sons.
- You are not a resource, you are Sons.
- There is nothing called fate for Child of God. It is called way.
- Children's minds are God's creative world, don't pollute it.
- Every word is a child (baby).
- Marriage is for goodness of Life, child birth is for peace and the child gives you joy.
- Your desire is your children(blessing).
- Unless you are a good partner to your children, you cannot be a good parent to them.

***

PRAISE

Enter his gates with thanksgiving; go into his courts with praise. Give thanks to him and praise his name. For the Lord is good. His unfailing love continues forever, and his faithfulness continues to each generation. ~ Psalms 100:4-5 NLT

Everything on earth will worship you; they will sing your praises, shouting your name in glorious songs. ~ Psalms 66:4 NLT

Praise

- Lift your voice of praise, not your noise of praise.
- If you fail to praise, you are failing your Life.
- When we praise, we set free other's bondages.
- When you are in complete joy, praise will run immeasurably through your body, mind and soul.
- Praise alone Befits the Benefits from the Lord.
- When a person is not able to praise God 1000 times more than his next person then he is the selfish person.
- Nobody can praise God heartfully when they are stuck, but praises flow when they are awestruck.
- To praise the Lord is our will, some do that some deny that.
- Praise empowers the performance of a prayer; peace emphasizes the presence of the prayer.
- Never murmur about your present for someone else is facing the toughest time of His Life. Let's thank God and praise Him every second for our present and future is safe in His Hand. Rejoice!

- Never try to be the king of the jungle, but be the King of Judah, the tribe that unceasingly praises and glorifies the marvelous works of God.
- Praise begins the positive thoughts; joy beckons victory.
- Praise is positive.
- Delayed praise is deadly.
- When your tongue is dry it cracks and it starts speaking unnecessary things. Keep it wet with praise.
- The responsibility for a man to praise God makes him a champion.
- When you want to praise, shut your ears.
- Praise makes you pregnant.
- Don't make your praise a debt.
- When you start to praise, you will never cease to praise.
- Praise is not worship; praise belongs to Him.
- No more action, everything becomes reaction when you praise.
- Limitless praise makes the curse useless.
- Don't invite the spirits by letting the evil spirit praise you.
- People will change when the seasons shift, but the true worshiper will always seek the Father's face.
- Work is not worship and nothing should be worshipped except the Creator.
- Celebrate the creations and worship the Creator.

- A powerful heart of worship will have unlimited pour of Spirit.
- Worship in Spirit & Truth and Rest in Peace.
- A church that obeys and worships without ceasing will never be cast out of His glory.
- Christian worship should not ENTERTAIN but EDIFY.
- Your worship cannot be customized.
- Worship is like a breath; create your own worship.
- Worship should be new every day and you should be passionate about it.
- Your worship is not a time for you to persist.
- Power of thanks overcomes the danger of death.
- Thanksgiving increases our strength.
- Don't fail God by not thanking Him.
- Power of Thanks is greater than death.
- Jesus Christ is the visible thanks that any man could see.
- Come swiftly to His presence with a Joyful Heart of Thanksgiving.
- If you don't thank God, you are a traitor.
- Don't let someone demean God by demanding a song from someone.
- Celebrate your Life to celebrate Christ.
- Don't compare yourself with other people. Just celebrate God.

- You can enjoy the creations but celebrate the Creator.
- To shut out the timid thoughts, shout for joy.
- Your joy should impact others.
- Joy is God made and not bound to a season.
- People want to enjoy and don't want to be in joy.
- Spirit is joy related.
- The unseen blessings are not pending but are on duty to prepare you to enjoy the complete fruit.
- Joy in heaven is interest free.
- The greatest gift by the person who cannot be separated from you is joy and it is of the Holy Spirit.
- Decide and reside in the unshakeable joy.
- The joy of the Holy Ghost adds strength to the weak and meek.
- Holy Spirit is not spirit of sorrow but Spirit of joy.
- Joy leads to the Father directly.
- Joy is not sin, anything that stops your joy is sin.
- God's blessings are a bundle of joy.
- Popularity kills the enjoyment.
- Joy is giving not receiving.
- If you are preaching about joy, do it Joyfully.
- You are a mighty vessel of God to perform miracles and to unfold the truth in so many lives. Give way for joy and be in it forever.

- Worry can never bring victory, joy can.
- Stop complaining and depending upon someone's chances for your joy.
- If you see Jesus in the things Holy Spirit shows you, you will be filled with the light called Joy.
- When you speak the right word given by the Spirit, you can enjoy the blessings.
- Jesus is never a threat to joy.
- Not every altar is of God.

***

SALVATION

There is salvation in no one else! God has given no other name under heaven by which we must be saved. ~ Acts of the Apostles 4:12 NLT

For here is the way God loved the world—he gave his only, unique Son as a gift. So now everyone who believes in him will never perish but experience everlasting life. ~ John 3:16 TPT

Salvation

- The Creator God, can forgive any sin.
- Forgiveness is the greatest sense of cleansing.
- Roar against the sin and not the sinner.
- It's a sin to doubt God.
- Talk to God so that you will not lease your body to sin.
- Disobedience is the greatest sin.
- Holiness inside you should be compatible even for a sinner to become holy.
- Salvation can digest sins.
- Jesus was a friend of sinners but not sins.
- Your character without Christ is a sin.
- When you walk in spirit you don't know what sin is.
- Worry is the greatest sin.
- The comparison is between righteousness and sin, not holiness and sin.
- Don't commit sin by omitting the voice of Holy Spirit.
- A mentally disabled person can't sin.

- If you tell God what you have done for Him, it becomes sin.
- Cleansing process is to be kept in secret.
- Don't sigh with the sins. Reign with the Righteousness.
- When sin gets full strength on you, death is certain.
- Sin is an act against God and He puts away them at will.
- Inheritance is a gift; lusting is a sin.
- Repentance is a process, it's not a number.
- Salvation doesn't have an expiry date.
- The relation between creation and salvation is a beautiful motivation.
- Salvation is savings.
- If you don't believe in creation, believe in salvation.
- Don't share the salvation with pigs.
- Salvation is Celebration!!! Don't look around and be sad, you are saved and that's not a token for someone's throne It's the key for your own kingdom, let the Spirit of gladness clothe you.
- Perfect salvation personified on the cross.
- Raise your eyes to the Cross of Calvary, you will find Heaven.
- You don't become Christian when you walk into a church, you become one when you walk with your cross in this society.

- Thinking about the backstabbers is such a waste of time. Think About the cross you will stay forward.
- Calvary is not your end, Mount Olives should be your beginning and your end.
- Reverse your hurts to know the truths.

***

PRAYERS

Pray in the Spirit at all times and on every occasion. Stay alert and be persistent in your prayers for all believers everywhere. ~ Ephesians 6:18 NLT

You draw near to those who call out to you, listening closely, especially when their hearts are true. Every godly one receives even more than what they ask for. For you hear what their hearts really long for, and you bring them your saving strength. ~Psalms 145:18-19 TPT

Prayer

- You are an answered prayer and no more you will be called sorrow.
- An absolute prayer is to pray for someone's prayer to be answered.
- A word of prayer – Jesus.
- Prayer cannot be procedural.
- Prayer is powerful, anyone can pray and receive the answers. If it's not happening, check to whom you prayed.
- Prayer is not just an answer. It's an answer with an action.
- Prayer is knowing, accepting and acknowledging the will of God.
- Prayer is a space to redeem yourself and refine your spirit.
- Jesus is my prayer partner.
- Prayer is not a challenge.
- A prayer can never die.
- Prayer is not just a compassion from God, it's a companion from God.
- Your soul is your prayer partner.

- Prayer in Spirit is effective than prayer in senses.
- Successful prayer is aligning with the will of God.
- Breathe prayer, pray like your breath.
- Prayer is not a compassion but a communion with God.
- When you join hands in prayer, you join hands with the Father.
- Your prayer is Father's time for you.
- Make your prayers as hearing not asks.
- Offer yourself first and the fiscal of Heaven will never run dry on you.
- We can fly in offer tickets, but to have the view of Heaven is divine.
- Offering should be offered often.
- Offering is never a onetime event, but an everyday moment.
- We don't expect men to put an offering, we want men to be the offering.
- Many boasts of their offerings, but the elite, sacrifice in secret.
- Don't fake your offerings.
- Offering is a lifestyle.
- Your offerings can be accepted by the Holy God only if it is holy.
- Father God never prays.

- When He is at your home, you need not pray, you just serve Him.
- It's a command not to worry about anything; pray without a worry.
- Prayers pays for years.
- If you want to celebrate the answer for your prayers, bless the answers.

***

MAXIM

So be very careful how you live, not being like those with no understanding, but live honorably with true wisdom, for we are living in evil times. Take full advantage of every day as you spend your life for his purposes. ~ Ephesians 5:15-16 TPT

Trust in the Lord with all your heart; do not depend on your own understanding. ~ Proverbs 3:5 NLT

Maxim

- Try not to teach anyone when they don't want you to be the one.
- Never compare earning to learning.
- Quit complaining before the queue inside your mind starts quarrelling.
- Honestly, humility is an adventure that takes you to the first.
- Jealousy is so lousy and noisy. Never spend time with her.
- Who's in your heart is the signature for what's on your mind.
- Quit complaining, quails will fall at your feet.
- This dying world needs no more lying words.
- Allow low inputs from all.
- Let your heart paint the picture.
- Hush and you will find the rush of the world.
- Speak to your problems and stop listening to it.
- God's warnings aren't curses but cautions.
- If you want to know the value of God sell yourself to God.

- If you are Loyal, you can be Royal.
- Give some season for the seed to grow.
- Think about whom you are contacting, whom you are dialing.
- Quit it before it quiets you.
- Care for others but don't crave for others.
- Speak in the Father's language.
- Wash your hearts and not hands.
- Remarks won't hurt you, regrets will.
- When you have decided to come to the presence of God, come running, don't stop.
- Have the Father's attitude.
- Don't carry a wrecked boat in your back.
- If you are lending your ears, you are learning their ways.
- There are choices you make in Life that are called decisions and most of the times these decisions make you. You are what you decided to be, so stop blaming and start living. Life is beautiful when you have no limitations and when you stop worrying about your future. Believe Life and it will lead you righteously.
- Inspiration leads to aspiration, so keep inspiring.
- Get inspired, don't goof around duplicating.
- Inspire to be 'New'.
- Talk with God and you will be kept away from enemy's lies.
- Your time of hike is now, climb as a conqueror.

- Remember the promise He made but more than that remind yourself who made that promise.
- Did pen worry about writing exams? Be the pen in God's hand.
- Be the answer not a reply.
- Stay strong, when you aren't wrong.
- When God makes you right, no one can pull you down from that height.
- The promise of God stays forever.
- Power over your poor fear.
- However Small or XL the battle might be, remember He is for us, not against us.
- Create your own copy of Him.
- Devil has two places: One is hell and the other is under your feet.
- Don't wish to be a high voltage electric line, it will be cut off when it becomes old. Be a line that powers your home.
- Diamonds will reflect at any angle you see it. Likewise, God will use you.
- You are an engager.
- An inspiration that comes from men will kill and destroy.
- If you are alive, you will raise people.
- If you know the presence of the Lord, you will make the problem lie in the presence of the Lord.
- Miracles never die.

- The words you speak will work if it is from God.
- Confidence will not work from outside but from inside.
- When devil tempts you for small things, God will create you a big circle.
- Do not be a member of the group, be a leader.
- Disciples are not discounted pieces, they are valuable sources but less used by the masters.
- Speak to the Mountains. Don't talk.
- We should be a new wine in the new cask.
- Desire the dress designed for you each new day.
- Build up on every opportunity.
- You be the message, don't wait for the message.
- Two wishes for Life: "To Love My LORD and to be Loved by my LORD."

**

CONFESSIONS

All who declare that Jesus is the Son of God have God living in them, and they live in God. ~ *1 John 4:15* NLT

The heart that believes in him receives the gift of the righteousness of God—and then the mouth confesses, resulting in salvation. ~ Romans 10:10 TPT

I will not die; instead, I will live to tell what the Lord has done. ~*Psalms 118:17* NLT

Daily Confessions

- I am fruitful, I am multiplying, I am increasing.
- I am highly favoured, I am highly respected, I am exceedingly loved.
- I am a Grace creature.
- I am blessed by His grace.
- Grace is my heartbeat.
- I am God's special treasure.
- I am happy, joyful and complete.
- I am not by chance but by choice.
- I am the living Church.
- I am a prophet to my life; I am a priest to my family.
- I am a king to the nations.
- My eyes are bright and will never become dull.
- I am healthy and have a sound mind.
- I have new thoughts of excellence.
- I am a new creation.

- Peace and prosperity is working for me today and forever from now.
- I resist the devil.
- I receive directly from Heaven.
- I lend to nations and not borrow.
- I am being resurrected.
- I am a word associated with Christ.
- I am a healthy person!
- I will not sin, I will be glorious.
- I am not there to impress anyone. I am there to express the glory of God.
- None can corrupt and touch me because God's vision is in me.
- He is my prophet for all season. He is a profit for all season.
- Thanksgiving is my dialect.
- My relationship with God is very present and pleasant.
- My mouth is a big treasure.
- I am close with God and I will never question him.
- I am more linguistic than the literate and am more legitimate than the legalised person.
- Only I can taste the answer of the prayer because I am the answer of the prayer.
- I am someone's prayer.

- I am here to create a generation of praise.
- Grace is reachable and I am teachable.
- I am a chapter of love; I am not a chapter of joke.
- I am the reflection of Jesus Christ.
- In Jesus, I am a Champion.
- When I am beside Jesus, I become a complete bride.
- I'm confident in Christ who promised me Eternal Life.
- I am the resting and dwelling place of the Father.
- I am the gospel of God.
- I am not obeying the Word of the Lord, I am being the Word of God.
- I am God's favorite word.
- I am a Son born of word.
- I was once a sinner, but now I am a Son.
- I am a person filled with His Spirit and nothing I do will go in vain.
- I am not gonna criticize the Spirit of God, I am gonna conquer the Spirit of God.
- I will create, but won't crave for someone's creation.
- I am a costly articraft of God.
- I am a miracle and I coexist with the miracle.
- Every sense in my body should just adore the presence of the Lord.

- I live my life the ordained way not the ordinary way.
- No grave can get hold of me.
- I am a healing balm.
- Healing is not a virtue. It is my right.
- His Grace remembers me.
- I'm washed by the blood of Christ and soaked in the love of Holy Spirit to keep me clean from the sin and dry from death.
- When I'm a beloved, I can never be a borrower.
- My Life will not be stagnant; I will flow, I will run after Holy Spirit.
- I should not be the threat but a treat to the kingdom of God.
- Heaven is where I belong and earth is where I'm being.
- My partner is Jesus and my finances are from Heaven.
- My spirit is free to explore.
- Holy Spirit is my time keeper.
- Holy Ghost is my wisdom.
- I abide and abode in Holy Spirit.
- Holy Spirit is my PR.
- Holy Spirit is my lover, He is my friend forever.
- My anointing is not behind gold, it grows gold.
- My feet aren't failures as my eyes of faith are on the Father.

- Famine is not mine. Flourishing is my flour of the meal.
- Prosperity is my identity.
- He makes me an undeniable testimony of prosperity.
- My blessings shall always bless me and never curse me.
- My blessings are fire proof and fire resistant.
- Blessings will always be my partner not my master.
- My money comes from my testimony about Him in me.
- I will be an unknown truth than an open lie to this beautiful world.
- I am the light and I will shine because I am the Son of the Saviour.
- I'm not here to defend God. He remains my defense forever.
- When I start to praise, I will never cease to praise.
- My praise is not greater than my Lord, My Lord is bigger.
- Praise is a commitment that I will never exalt anyone except Him.
- I don't have any debts on thanks.
- I'm a wine to yield the divine joy.
- My job is to enjoy what God has created.
- I am not an offering box in the temple; I am the Temple.
- I am His prized possession.
- I am happy Holy Spirit.

- I am a heavenly being and my payment comes from heaven.
- I am not a filthy water; I am a tasteful wine.
- There is no pressure in heaven and so I don't want anything that is not of heaven.
- He is the provider and giver of Full life.
- Lord, let me not keep a record of anyone who has wronged me.
- Glory be to God who restores my health like that of eagles.
- He is the living bread in my baskets. He is the living portion in my banquets.
- Insult is not an ingredient in my blessings.
- I love everybody who He loves.
- God has not given me a spirit of fear, insecurity, timidity, cowardness and self-image. But he has given me a Spirit of power, love, clear mind and self-discipline and many more righteous things. Amen

***

Personal Reflections

Personal Reflections

Personal Reflections

Personal Reflections

www.ingramcontent.com/pod-product-compliance
Lightning Source LLC
Chambersburg PA
CBHW050018170726
48282CB00025B/446
* 9 7 8 8 1 9 8 4 9 8 4 5 8 *